Ode

Samuel Gluck

Ode by Samuel Gluck

Email: hello@orenaugmountainpublishing.com
Website: www.orenaugmountainpublishing.com

ISBN: 979-8-9925369-9-7

The work herein was written in 2024 and 2025, and would not have been possible without the love, influence, support, and encouragement of Murielle, my muse and inspiration,

Or without the love of my family Alanna, Dana, and Linda,

Or without *Island Lady*, my first poem, the original of which is contained in these pages.

I am forever grateful to Sandy Carlson and Edward Dzitko
of Orenaug Mountain Publishing
for bringing Muse and Ode into reality.

Ode

Derived from a Greek word *aeidein*, which means to chant or sing.

A lyric poem in the form of an address to a particular subject, often elevated in style or manner, marked by exaltation of feeling typically of a serious or meditative nature.

An expression of a noble feeling with dignity, or a way or path written in celebration, appreciation, or dedication and often celebrating a person, place, or thing.

Author's Note

In these poems you might notice an absence of punctuation, except in cases where there is dialogue, and where it is necessary to be clear about the words being spoken in conversation rather than narration.

The omission of punctuation is meant to create or enhance ambiguity, emotion, urgency, visual impact and poetic license in order to allow the reader to interpret the poem through their eyes.

Several of these poems also appeared in *Muse*.

Table of Contents

Beauty is truth, truth beauty–that is all
Ye know on earth, and all ye need to know.

John Keats (1795-1821), English poet

Reverent

Reverent am I in the Temple of Embrace
In your presence I abide
Never will I hide from your face

Reverent am I in the Sanctuary of Soul
To be content within myself
safe complete and whole

Reverent am I in the Palace of Dawn
Under the canopy of your eye
To your flame am I drawn

Reverent am I in the Castle of Strength
My Guardian and Protector
throughout my time of distress

Reverent am I in the Kingdom of Kindness
A pillar of fire to lead me
through the desert of my darkness

Reverent am I in the Fortress of Faith
In the halo of the Holy
and the certainty of belief

Reverent am I at Heaven's Gate
In the luminosity of glory
in the presence of the Great

Reverent am I in the Throne of Love
To have a seat in the light
Showering from above

Reverent am I in the Creation of the Cosmic
To bask in the aura of the majestic
and the magic of the poetic

Ode to a Legend

Once I imagined I was a great poet
A Laureate
I won the Pulitzer Prize for lit
And the Nobel for bullshit

Before that I was a famous actor
And a Rock star
I won an Oscar and a Grammy
How uncanny

Before that I was a star athlete
I hit 100 home runs and
threw 100 touchdowns in the same year
What a career

Before that I was a little boy
Wondering what I would be when I grew up
"Dream Big" mommy would say
And mommies are always right

It's so wonderful that now I am all grown up
all of my dreams have come true
and that I became the legend of my mind
so that I can share my dreams with you

Ode to the Poet

The poet is a dreamer
A prophet of what might be
Speaking in rhyme or lyric
And the visions that he sees

The poet creates an image
Of a world to fit his imagery
Where life is peace and beauty
And all beings live in harmony

Yes the poet is a dreamer
And life is his dream
Like a painter with his canvas
Imagining scenes that are serene

Where he lives in his wishes
And sometimes they come true
But his bubble can burst broken
and he can wake up sad and blue

The angels have a lyre
And sing songs oh so sweet
And the devils light the fire
Of evil, malice, guile, and deceit

The poet is a dreamer
In a world of demons and ghouls
Where the wicked and cruel can flourish
And where tread sinners and fools

Does the poet ever know it
That his life is a fleeting dream
You can read all about it here
Where poets reign supreme

A Poem

A poem
a moment frozen
in time
made crystalline
held up to shine
through the rays of the sun
to see its refraction
into colored beams of light
each with an interpretation or insight
to see what it is
that we wish it to be
just like you, just like me.

A poem
an instant chosen
not to fade away
into the distant memory
but to always stay
as an ever present reality
an experience to be relived
in a moment's notice
to bring one nearest
to what is dearest
in the soul in the heart
not even death can tear it apart.

A poem
a time defined
into immortality
much more than a dream
that passes through the night
to be forgotten
but a glimpse of reality
caught in a split second of clarity
and seen with eyes wide open
on the screen of eternity
just like you, just like me.

Amino Acids

Amino acids in an ancient ocean
A long time ago
Joining uniting bonding
Forming complex chains
Dividing into cells–male/female
Growing developing into beings
Of movement instinct intelligence
The male swimming in darkness
A journey–the odds of surviving
So small–propelled by nature and destiny
To change into one new soul

Swimming now in clear waters
Separate and equal under sun and moon
Aquamarine shining are your eyes
Light surrounded by flesh
Immersed now in waters fresh
Grown cells–female/male–
Young old timeless
Light in your smile

Catch Me if You Can

What am I, and who are you
And what are you holding in your hand
Are your eyes moving your mind spinning
your heart feeling your spirit soaring
What is it exactly you are imagining

Am I a thought a mood
Insight or spark of spirit channeled by hand
Points of ink a string of letters
Arranged according to your random plan
Scattered lines on a page
Creating images or feelings to gauge
Be they silly petty profound or sage

I float through space time
The here and the now
The before and the after and beyond the beyond
I am in galaxies in black holes and all spaces in between
In quarks mesons and ions
in every soul I can be seen
In infinity and eternity I am unbound

If you try or believe
You might catch me if you can
Arrange me in any order
And come to understand
That I come not from you but in and through
I am that I am
You may catch me if you can

Destination

I was walking down the road one day
and nothing seemed the same
it seemed I had lost my way
I couldn't even remember my name
Night was falling and there I was stranded in the dark
so I decided to sit myself down on a nearby rock

Suddenly a stranger appeared
and I was taken aback
I didn't know where I was
or how to get back on track
I asked the stranger where I was
and he said to have no fear
"Son," he said, "I don't know where YOU are
but I know that I am here."

So I said, "I don't know what to do
or which way I should go
maybe you can set me straight
And point me to the right road."

"You could go right or to the left
so I don't know where you're heading
best to break right on through
and face whatever it is you are dreading
there's a door to a tunnel straight ahead
that will take you in your direction
It may be dark or may be bright
but might clear up your perception."

"Well how will I know where I'm going
if I don't have a map
Cause I lost my phone and I can't see
and I don't have that app?"

The stranger smiled and said, "Listen very carefully
to these words that will set you free
you may find loss
or you may find gain
you might have joy
or you may feel pain
but for this I'm sure
if you don't open that door
You will never find what it is
that you are looking for."

"Thank you kind sir,
for all your information.
Now I know what to do
and how to arrive at my destination."
And one more thing I asked
to the kind stranger:
"What is your name and thank you
for keeping me out of danger."

The stranger looked me in the eye
and said these words to me,
"You know who I am.
I am you and you are me
and our name is Sam."

Driving

When I was 16 Dad taught me how to drive
But before he would let me behind the wheel he taught me
How to change a flat tire
It's a good thing for a young man to have a skill
and be self-reliant

When I got behind the wheel the first thing
Dad taught me was to look into the rearview mirror
It's important to know what is happening in front of you
"keep your eyes on the road"
"Look straight ahead"
"Keep your eyes on the goal"
But just as,if not more important,
 is to be aware of what is not in front of your eyes

Ever since, the rearview mirror is permanently implanted in my brain,
And the farther I travel down the road, the larger it becomes

Sometimes I get lost and I'm not so sure where I'm heading,
But it sure is clear where I'm coming from
Thanks Dad

Force Magnetic

Is that what you felt when my pixels formed on your screen
And your finger went click
A force magnetic
Is that what you recognized when we met face to face
And you smiled
A force electric
Is that what you wanted when I sat next to you
The first time
A force kinetic
Is that what you longed for when you came to my place
And never left
A force volcanic
Is that what you feel in our embrace
every day and every night
In the dark or by the dawning light
Skin on skin mouth on mouth
Limbs entwined minds that shine
Face to face eye to eye
Heart to heart soul to soul
In our warmth and out from the cold
Do you ever wonder why
The force majestic

Ephemeral

I look around and everything seems so ephemeral
As if reality is composed of pixels or bits of matter
suspended in air

I've had a couple dozen cars
Some very fast and sporty
Others practical and economical

and I have lived in as many locations,
sometimes for a couple of months, or for decades.
But wherever I was
Here I AM

I've had hundreds of outfits, styles, fashions
and looks that seem to come and go
But I always seem to find myself in a pair of jeans
Thank you Levi Strauss

I look at my friends those who are still around
And wonder WTF happened to you?
Of course, I'm the same as I used to be
I haven't changed a bit
Just an older version of my younger self,
becoming who I used to be but better

I've been with so many women
I can't even remember their names
Some got away and others I let go
I've even had a couple of wives
One gave me the greatest gift
The other cut me with a knife
After all I have had, lost, and lived through
What is most important is a love that is true
someone to hold near and close through the night

Everything else is just ephemera

Flight 7890

Attention all passengers
Flight 7890 will be boarding at the gate
No need to worry no need to rush
It is always on time you won't be late

Your booking is confirmed
And your first class seat is reserved
You are sure to receive the service
and the courtesy that you most assuredly deserve

Your plane is fueled, ready and waiting
And will be taking off soon
Maybe this month, perhaps next year
or possibly tomorrow by noon

On board are people of all ages
Though most appear to be elderly
Some may be known and seem familiar
there are even several famous celebrities

The crew have made this trip many times before
And are very kind and professional
They seem to have wings and act angelic
And the pilot's name is Captain Gabriel

You will be greeted upon your arrival
With festivities for all of your fellow travelers
A great party awaits you In a beautiful palace
filled with blissful happy revelers

Attention Flight 7890 will be boarding soon
For arrival at your permanent vacation
Calling all passengers Flight 7890 is ready for takeoff
departing soon for your final destination

Safe travels
See you on the other side

Ode to the Fruit of the Vine

When I was young I had an unquenchable thirst
to drink the finest wines
I was intoxicated by the thrill of the search
for the ultimate Fruit of the Vine

I went to France and there I drank
from the wines of Burgundy
I tasted a full bodied bordeaux a juicy chardonnay
and a sweet blonde named chablis

C'est magnifique I was told
but my search was incomplete
So I decided that I had to taste
the fine wines of Italy

I was very tired and oh so hungry
Thirsty dry beyond compare
The sky was so blue the sun so hot
but I really did not care

I stopped at a lovely vineyard
by a beautiful Tuscan field
Dreaming that my search would bear fruit
and that my desire would soon yield

When suddenly she appeared
a golden goddess with lips red like wine
I was taken aback when she asked
"Are you looking for the fruit of the vine"?

I had never before seen such beauty
a completely unexpected surprise
I thought I was drunk and out of my mind
and I could not believe my eyes

"I've been waiting for you I know what you need
and I can give you the very best"
Then she came close and put my mouth
on her beautiful succulent breast

Drink my love from a heart that's true
because you deserve the absolute best
And so I drank to my heart's content
and know that I am truly blessed

When I awoke she was gone
then I knew my search was complete
The finest wine comes not from the vine but from a heart of love that
is true and sweet

Ode to a Garden of Love

In the garden of love
Grows the flower of light
A reflection of the eternal
The clear the great and the bright
Not touching fertile Earth
Still felt so deep
So beautiful to sight
It's scent so sweet
Not nourished by rain
But of itself sustained

In the garden of pure love
Grows the flower of light
Shimmering and effulgent
In the day or at night
Rooted to Earth or floating in sky
Ever present in the mind or to the eye
Revealed to all who open the heart
In the garden of love
The flower of light can never die

Ode to a Heart

Ode to thee dear heart of mine
You have lived within me before my birth
Without your constant beat
I would not have survived
And you have given me
a truly wonderful life

Quiet and still you know
what my mind can never fathom
You know my innermost feelings
And deepest dark secrets
Which you bring to light
When my mind is silent

May you live in tranquil harmony
So that your beauty and wisdom
Will be reflected and shine through me
May you have a serene and steady rhythm
Peace is your mantra

OM SHANTI OM SHANTI OM SHANTI

Ode to a Man

I am a human being
Created in the image of God
I am a man
Of this there is no doubt
Determined by countless generations which preceded me
and by chromosomes named X and Y
I am a man
I know this to be the truth by looking in the mirror
And pleased with who is looking back at me
I greet each day grateful to be alive and thankful that
I am a man
I recognize the female within me as I am a
Reflection of my mother who bore me
By my sisters who adored me
And by the women who have loved me because
I am a man
I am a son
I honor my father and my mother who gave me
The gift of life and raised me to know that
I am a man
I am a soul
Which is eternal surrounded and embodied in flesh
Which is constantly changing as does all creation
I am a man
I know the light in my eyes and the light in the sun is the same Light
The space within me and the space without
is the space in which I am
Because I know that
I am a man

I am an energy field
I have the power to attract and repel and will manifest into my reality
That which I desire because
I am a man

I had a beginning which is called birth
And I will have an end which is known as death
Everything in between is the gift of life
I know this to be the ultimate truth and I have no fear
I am a man

I Am Waiting

I am waiting
Desperately waiting for you
For something or someone
to come through
from beyond the blue

I am waiting
I have always been waiting
Thinking of what I have to do
What must be done
for me to get through

What was it that I was waiting for?
Was it the thrill of the unexpected or unknown
The coming of whatever was "next"
While everyone else was content
In their comfort zone and "getting ahead"
I was chasing tail and "getting head"

For what am I waiting?
Waking to the morning sun
The day to come
The Messiah

I am waiting

The Iron Dome

There is an Iron Dome in the sky
The Shield of David covers his kingdom
While the enemies of Zion
Prepare their swords and bows
And sharpen their arrows
and weapons of war

Like Orks they prepare a pit
and tunnels in the ground
to bury the children of The Nova
Into which they fall
with extreme vengeance
Nasrallah Sinwar and Hanniyah
And all the acrid agents of malevolence
Hamas and Hezbollah martyred to Allah

The Almighty Lord of Hosts
He Who dwells most high
Destroyer of the false and the wicked
With thunder lightning and fire
All the evildoers and the speakers of lies
Those who worship death shall perish
And those who love life shall thrive
There is an Iron Dome in the sky

Amen

Highway I-95

The road of life is such a trip
what a blast being alive

I don't want this ride to end
Unless it is for a brand new drive
Like taking a trip on highway I95

What comes after
Do re mi fa so la ti do
or after you pass go
What comes after the color violet
New colors and new sounds
new roads to be found

If there are colors that cannot be seen
And sounds which cannot be heard
Maybe there is a path to pastures more green
or a road to some higher ground

Like going from here to there
Or from there to here
It's better to be anywhere
And to be free and in the clear

I don't wanna die So I'll just fade away
Like a flower falling into the ground
Or today becoming yesterday
Like a bubble bursting on a pond
Or a song after the last note sounds

I'll just get myself a brand-new car
And go on an all new drive
I'm not sure where I'm going
But I'm feeling totally alive
It will be a gas taking another trip
on highway I-95

Island Lady

My ship is entering your harbor island lady
my anchor is plunging heavily headlong
into the soft sandy bottoms of your bay
and I am coming to stay awhile
on your tropical isle
of setting suns and orange skies
moonstruck nights and star shine eyes
of blue violet and purple moons
hanging over lazy lagoons
and your slender palms pulsating in the evening breeze
rustling through the leaves and through your hair
like the breath of a shadow

You are as lovely in the darkness
as you are brilliant in the light
island lady make love with me tonight
live totally in this moment that will last us for a life
make our time tonight timelessly infinite
and let me live forever in your mind and heart
just as I live in every part
of your luscious island home
Just as you've made your way deeply into my soul

Ode to the Lady of the Isle

Ode to thee fairest Lady of the Isle
I haven't seen you in a long long long while
You live now only on the island of my dreams
enchanted was I by your look and your smile

I dreamt you into my reality
Then you appeared like a glorious vision
A portent of what was to come
the physical embodiment of an ethereal apparition

You entered into the sultry tropical night like a phantasm
And I was blown away in the wake of your vibration
Your sky blue eyes, long dark hair and lucent white skin
A masterpiece curated by a celestial magician

You read Kabbalah and The Tibetan Book of the Dead
Threw tarot cards and knew the I Ching
You were my tantric teacher my spiritual guide
and taught me many wonderful mystical things

We undulated under the swaying palms
Our love was exotic, erotic to the sound of soft Pacific waves
Your smile your grace was the radiant frame
Around your beauteous face

We slept beneath the stars on a beach of golden sand
And lived on coconuts and avocado
We were enraptured and free as the ocean breeze
You were my Venus and I your Apollo

Had we stayed on our tropic isle of
setting suns and moonstruck nights
We will never know what might have been
We were shooting stars sparkling in the dark night sky
I will see you in Paradise Island Lady
where we will be together again

Kind and Loving

Be kind and loving
Please don't be angry or pout
Be soft and forgiving
No need to yell, no need to shout

Be soft and gentle
Please never distant or cold
Put a smile on your face
Don't grimace, don't scold

Love is the juice
That we all want to drink
Always sweet never bitter
Lifts the heart or we sink

Be kind and loving
With that shine in your eye
Like the sun melting snow
Lustrous, bright and high in the sky

Melancholy with a Side

Hello Old friends
Melancholy and Nostalgia
I haven't seen you around in a while
Then again I've been busy
You know with Life and stuff like that

You used to be my pals, my constant companions
Now I barely recognize you
except maybe at the end of winter
When everything looks so gloomy
It's a good thing Spring follows

You would sound good on a menu
Next time I'll order some Melancholy
Sounds like a new vegetable,
a cross between a melon and cauliflower
With a little melodrama thrown in for some extra spice
Steamed, roasted, broiled or with rice
with a side of Nostalgia
All for the right price

Just for old times sake
Like when we used to go to the corner deli
And get a hot dog for 25 cents

See ya around old friends

No Matter

No matter what my age
I am life
As long as I can sit
In the light of the sun
And merge with The One

As long as my breath moves
Like the waves of the ocean
I am in my home
I sway with the wind
In the ebb and the flow

No matter how my body may change
As long as I can move I am free
I can never be caged
I am sine qua non
I am in the One

Ode to a Cup

Oh wouldst that I were able
to have a seat at thy table
To drink contently from thy cup
with breakfast lunch and sup
to taste thy wine so fine
and quench this thirst of mine.

Oh wouldst that I were able
to share a seat at thy table
and taste thy fruits so sweet
Oh would thee I entreat
I'd ravage thy cupboards bare
such delicacies beyond compare
and gladly return for more
for thy endless bounty would restore.

Oh wouldst if I were able
to lay my plate upon thy table
Will this hunger not abate
for a morsel a piece a taste
Will my cup go unfilled
Say you will... Say you will
Oh wouldst that I were able
to fill my cup upon thy table.

Ode to a Banquet

A banquet is prepared for me, with fine wine
    you restored my heart
        when I was empty, and made me shine

I know this to be true because it is as clear
    as the full moon glistening through the night,
        and because our hearts are full and rejoice

Our laughter is pure, joyful
    like the sound of champagne
        pouring into a glass, or water falling on stone

I have no fear because together
    we are stronger than an oak,
        or an unbreakable bone

Though the dark nights may be long
    the light of dawn shines through your face
        Your voice is like a bird singing her morning song

Our love is sweet like ripe fruit,
    sensuous, soft and succulent,
        Sumptuous, luscious

A banquet has been prepared and you are delicious,
I am sated, my thirst abated, my cup runneth over
        I hunger no more It is you I desire and adore

Ode to a Lion

Ode to thee ruler monarch of the wild
Great is your glory long shall you reign
Your fame is enduring so magnificent to sight
Known to all as the King Leo is his name

Awesome and brave without peer
The undisputed lord of beasts
Praises to your fame and majesty
Throughout time will never cease

Your royal coat is golden
Your majestic mane is your crown
Forever fearless always noble
Ruler of all who roam the ground

May you mate with your pride
And spread your indomitable seed
Would be challengers to your fearsome roar
must bow and humbly concede

Your presence is enthralling
You are the animal kingdom's crown jewel
To each and every beast in the wild
Odes and praises King Leo forever may you rule

Ode to a Lioness

Ode to thee fairest lioness of the field
Glories and praises to thee
my heart I do yield

Your beauty and grace is known to all
Humbled and honored am I
in your presence I crawl

Privileged am I and blessed to share
A place by your side
to bed in your lair

In the thrill of the hunt I witness your skill
And wonder in awe
as you go for the kill

Potent and powerful Queen apex feline
as long as I am king
you will be mine

Ode to a Greek Goddess

Like Aphrodite Athena and Artemis
I have seen a golden Greek goddess
Statuesque graceful strong and firm
I look into her eyes and see stars shine
I look to the moon and see spirit fly
I look to the ground and see her run
Fleet swift strong
It is her nature an intuition
Like an unseen river deep underground
A powerful current the sound
I can feel her come
Roaring to merge with the ocean

Ode to Day and Night

Hello again and to you a Good day
My oldest and dearest friends
Hope you had a peaceful rest
I am so happy to see you again

Thank you for the sweet dream
My lovely lady of the night
You are my warmest comfort
Who wakes me to each new morning delight

What a joy to be blessed
with such wonderful friends
to live a life filled with adventure
and know a love that transcends

The heat of the sun
Or the cold of the dark
To enjoy my many great friends
In the land of my dreams and then to embark

Out of my dream again to awake
Into the new dawn I so humbly pray
For a peaceful sleep and another good night
And please God for a brand-new day

Ode to Life

Ode to thee dear friend of Life
My soul has been restored
Thank you for all your gifts
And for the many blessings bestowed

Praise to thee dear rising sun
And the glorious power of your light
I look forward to greeting you again
With the wisdom of your insight

Even in my dreams you are always by my side
We travel to places never before seen
with people and loves both known and lost
so I can be with them   again and again

Dearest companion of this Life
You have been my closest friend
And I know you will go on without me
When our time together comes to its end

Then you will be with all those whom I love
And I know you will love them as sweetly
As you have loved me
Dear friend of life thank you for loving me so deeply

Ode to Love

Ode to thee dearest love of life
What would I do what would I be without you
Could I live would I die
or merely exist

You fill me with the food of life
breath, earth and sky
Like a flower turning to the sun
I bask in your light my dearest one

You assume many forms and take different shapes
At times you are a goddess or sometimes a child
You might be a friend or a beast in the wild
Always you are beautiful

You might be a bird singing in a tree
Or the stars sparkling in the sky
when the moon rises
from out of the sea

At times I thought you were forever lost
I was in grief, despair and bereft
I feared I would never see you again
But truly you never left

You were within me all the time
A seed waiting to flower again
It only required a clearer view
so that I could more deeply know you

Oh dear love what would I be
What could I do without you
Could I live would I thrive
Without you I truly am not fully alive

Ode to thee dearest love of life

Ode to Spring (Or a Romantic Spring Fever)

Ode to thee fair maiden of spring
Praises of love to thee I do sing
Your trees now in blossom your fields turning green
Honored and awed am I by your beauty just seen

Sweet lily fair lilac dearest flower of purple
You make my soul quiver you make my heart gurgle
Your petals so lovely so exquisite your scent
Such beauty to behold a sensual intoxicant

So soft is thy belly so full is thy breast
My face my head I pray on thee may I rest
May I climb on thy mountains and lay in thy valleys
My rivers my streams join in the blue of thy seas

In the dark of the night my love calleth to me
Neither shadows nor dreams can block the light that I see
Our bodies touch our mouths again meet
So total the comfort our kisses so sweet

United embraced into each other we melt
So familiar it seems so deeply love felt
The greatest gift just given separate lives made whole
You fulfilled my self you restored my soul

Now knowing the truth which was recently guessed
No longer a wonder our minds now at rest
Dearest maiden of spring my cup runneth over
Sweet lily fair lilac wilt thou beest my lover

Ode to Sunrise

Out of the darkness
The saga continues
The birth of each new day
brings fresh colors and hues

Out of the black
Comes the luminous morning light
A breathtaking revelation
Miraculous to the sight

Light is ever present
Only the darkness is brief
To show humanity the way
Through mortal pain sorrow and grief

As the seasons change
So will the time of your rise
Always will I wait in wonder
And gaze up at the skies

Your Light is clear eternal
Forever permanent and omnipresent
Great almighty light of day
Shining brilliant glowing incandescent

Ode to a Butterfly

Ode to thee fairest Monarch of Spring
Your colors so vibrant such a beautiful thing
You float through the air bringing beauty to my world
Such a thrill to behold your glory unfurled

Though your reign may be short on your wings may I fly
And paired as your escort may we soar to the sky
You flutter on a flower you make my eyes shine
Turning my garden and world into a shrine

May your beauty forever reign throughout the summer heat
Bringing joy and wonder and making life so sweet
Always bringing delight and a smile to my face
As you gently rise and float away in space

Reign on fairest monarch of summer and spring
Odes and praises to thee forever will I sing
May your beauty flourish your luster never fade
Forever will I wonder just how you were made

Ode to Rain

The heavens are bursting and
Our dear Earth is thirsting Great Father Sky
Is inseminating Mother Earth
With his life giving rain
Bringing forth new birth

Your fresh waters are surging
Through rivers brooks and streams
As heavily oxygenated blood is gushing
Through my arteries and veins
Like your life giving rain

You can fall too hard
Like a punch from a fist
Or drop so softly like a fine mist
You can wash away all my dirt all my shame
Erase my guilt and ease all my pain

Dear life giving rain
When you fall too much we complain
Too little and we struggle in vain
Grant me your awesome power to grow
All mighty life giving rain

Ode to a Kiss (or The Power)

The power of your kiss
Is like a sudden earthquake
Makes my knees shake
rolling rocks can not break

The power of your touch
Is like the softest rain
Eases away all my pain
leaves nothing to explain

The power of your look
Takes my breath away
Makes my head spin
like the wild west wind

The power of your embrace
Brings a gentle softness to my face
Makes my tensions dissipate
is soft and tender like fine lace

The power of your smile
Shines bright as the evening star
Plays like a soulful sultry song
from the strings of my guitar

The power of your heart
Is like a volcanic eruption
Spewing hot molten flows
of passions and emotions

The power of your love
Is a kind gentle presence
Sent on the wings of angels
A gift from above the heavens

Ode to Light

Ode to thee light of my Life
I open my eyes and am greeted by sunlight
More than the absence of darkness
You reveal what is true in plain sight

You illuminate the way and enable me to see
When before I was blind
True light is self effulgent
your waves illuminate my mind

Great Lord of Infinite Light
Grant me the vision of your perfect insight
the gift to see the real and the bright
The blessings of my birthright

You are electromagnetic incandescent
Laser focused and diffused
ultraviolet infrared or gamma
by your light my soul is infused

Ode to a Waterfall

Waterfall may we stand by your flowing waters
    May we sit by your cool mist
       Immersed in your soft spray
         Surrounded in your sweet sound

 May we drink from your sacred source
    Sustained in your super strength
      Nourished we thrive awake and alive
     We are in you waterfall

Not afraid am I
    of being swept away
      by the rush of your force
Though your currents
    may at times be rough
      I know you will lead me to still waters
       I know that in your kiss we flow
        into the sacred ocean of bliss

     Waterfall may we
      stand by your
       flowing waters

Ode to the Waveless Ocean

Floating on the waveless ocean
Or surfing the movements of mind, I find
That being tossed by the ebbs and flows
Of the changing tides might be keeping me blind

In stillness, the fog of illusion
evaporates in the light of the morning sun,
The daily journey has begun
To unite in the One

The never ending flow of thoughts and dreams
Is like sitting on the side of a river or stream,
Watching everything coming and going
Isn't always as it seems

The layers of dense clouds clear
Revealing the endless depths
Of the infinite glow of love
Floating on the light of the waveless ocean

Ode to a Pee

I think that I shall never see
Such a wonder as my pee
I never know when it will come
But surely I will have to run
To find the nearest bush or tree
Hoping no one will find me
Or maybe I'll have to pull off the road
Hoping I won't suddenly explode
Or maybe a cop will take me to jail
And tell me I should just get a pail
I used to flow like a strong young horse
But then Father time took its course
I'll wake up in the middle of the night
Twice or thrice before daylight
I used to flow like the Niagara Falls
But now when nature calls
I'm just an old man who has to pee
My god-damn prostate is getting the best of me

Ode to the Coming and the Going

Hey How is it going?
How are you coming along?

Everything is in the coming and the going
Either in the reaping or the sowing

Everything is in the making
Or already happened
Like the present becoming yesterday
Or tomorrow becoming today

Everything is in the coming and the going
The joy and the pain the loss and the gain
There is no reason to complain
So why rack your brain

Everyone is in the birthing or the dying
Or maybe reliving
Everything and everyone
Is coming and going from The Being

Ode to Sand Dunes

Sand dunes dance away with the wind
 They change their shape
  To its every whim

While turquoise white-capped waves
 Whip endlessly against
  Black volcanic crags
   On the ocean of time

Gushing falls rush tumultuously
 Towards wispy wet deep glades
  They shake and they sway
   And ebb at their bay

While falling rains drop softly like
 Tears of joy on a shallow pool
  Their ripples reflecting
   The light of it all

Rising Lion

There is a lion rising out of the land
Leaping lions across the desert sands
Winged lions flying high in the skies
      hurling thunder, lightning and raining fire
Invisible lithe and nimble like a cat
      powerful strong and invincible in combat

Lethal lions will defend their pride
Fighting lionesses protect the tribe

Raging lions by the light of day
Angels in heaven are leading the way
Angry lions by dark of night
Lions of Judah ready to fight

Pharaoh met his end at the Red Sea
Ayatollah's days will end in misery

The Shield of David Is our might
The God of Israel is by our side

Ode to the Seed of Love

A seed of love
Carried on the softest breath
From the cosmic wind
Could have blown away
Washed away into oblivion
Leaving not the mark of a speck of dust
Ever to be seen by the naked eye
Human or otherwise

Ever so subtly to take root
Gently and tenderly
Seemingly invisibly
Through cycles and seasons
Passing perhaps for eons
A chance conception an interminable gestation
An act of procreation
A birthing in love making

A beginning an ending a changing
The wheel of karma inevitably turning
Transforming reshaping time and space
For the earthly seedlings

Siddhartha

In my beginning, I was a prince in the tribe of my birth
and I dwelled in the Temple of Learning

I came of age and I opened the Doors of Perception to
climb the Ladder of Sacred Divination

To the Dharma, in the pure land, and so began my search
for the noble path to Nirvana Samadhi Moksha

I met yogis gurus mystics and sadhus
SwamiJi YogiJi and Bhaktivedanta Swami

I channeled my energies through the chakras,
to the rise of Kundalini to become healthy happy and holy

I lived in ashrams temples and Zen retreats
and learned asana mudra kriya and bandha

I chanted Om Namo Shivaya
and sang Hare Krishna Hare Rama

I was brahmacharya I created no karma
I was blissed out

I surfed on waves of prana and tamed the wild beasts of tantra,
I developed siddhis I became a Yogi

And the women came like moths drawn to the flame
Once The life force was released it was impossible to restrain

Like wild horses they could not be contained,
I strayed, became selfish and foolish and wandered
in wanderlust for years, through tears

To the Land Flowing with Milk and Honey
Where I fell under the spell of a beauty wearing Gucci

I was dazzled and beguiled by her glamour and style
and at times it was sweet, but it ended in betrayal and deceit

My heart was in shock I was running out of breath
I found myself laying in the valley of the shadow of death

I remembered the words from the Temple of Learning
from where I began a gentle voice whispered

"Have No Fear" and I awoke
I was restored made whole

I came to a place with green pastures and still waters
Calm restored to my soul

A woman of valor was waiting for me,
Never again will I wander nor a reason to roam

Peace is in my heart love is in my home
Hare OM

    I Am Siddhartha

Sorry I'm Late

Sorry I'm late, I just saw a dog
I stopped for a while
To watch the sun melt the fog

Sorry I'm late, I just saw a deer
It took a little time
to get over my fear

Sorry I'm late I just saw a fox
It takes a lot of time
To think out of the box

Sorry I'm so late I just saw a bear
It took all of my time
To fix and style my hair

Ode to My Spirit Wolf

My spirit wolf comforts me
He watches over me through the night
My guardian protector through the darkness
The bringer of the morning light

My spirit wolf teaches me
To be always aware and remain free
He plays with me like a child
And opens my eyes so I can see

My spirit wolf talks to me
From his mind and through his heart
He forever will live inside of me
We will never ever part

My spirit wolf

The Future

I live in the future now
SpaceX rockets are zooming
To the space station
and soon to the moon and Mars

Electric cars drive by themselves
And AI tells me all I need to know
So I don't have to go to school anymore
because they don't teach anything anyway

Soon we won't have to work
Because our robots will do everything for us
I'll name mine Chris or Pat so it can decide
What gender it wishes to be any time
Why not?

Everyone is healthy now
And we can get new hips and knees
And even a new face
Soon we will be able to transfer
our brains into a brand new body
It will be like getting a new car
I can't wait!

There is no war anymore
That is so twentieth century
Everyone is kind and peaceful
and there is hate no more

Racism is so over
So 1950's
It doesn't matter if you are
Yellow tan brown or black
Unless you are an evil toxic rich white male oppressor colonizer
Not to mention stealing everything from everyone everywhere forever
Peace and love soul brother
I love you too Brown Sugar

We are all so happy and peaceful now
No more acrimony or ill feelings
And everyone is rich and no one is broke
thanks to our wonderful government
Which gives us free money
So we will vote for them forever
It really pays to be Woke
No joke

And we finally elected a woman president
Of course she is a woman of color
She used to be a man
But he woke up
If it works in sports
Why not in politics
it's just a game anyway

We don't need borders anymore
Because we're just one big happy family
What is mine is yours and what is yours is mine
And if you don't have anything neither should I
because that would be so unfair

Welcome to the future everyone everywhere
I used to watch the Jetsons
But now life is so mucho much mo better than ever
I'm so happy that I live in the future
And all my dreams have come true

Ode to Time

What is time?
The Sun rising and falling
The earth spinning on its axis
The earth revolving around the sun
Galaxies spinning in the vast distances of space

What is time?
Shadows on a dial facing the sun
Sands falling through two glass bulbs
Two hands slowly rotating around numbers
Digitized points of light on an electronic device

What is time?
More valuable than diamonds gold or money
An incessant stream constantly flowing
A gateway to the past, or into the future
And ever present, but any attempt to grab
onto will slip through your fingers
Chapters in the book of life
Rented from the overlord
A bird that flies by
Time is
up

Ode to Twinkle Twinkle

Twinkle twinkle little star
Jack and Jill fell down the hill
Mary lost her little lamb
And now I have to take my pill

Red Riding Hood met Goldie Locks at the
nursing home by granny's house
Little Boy Blue lost his mind
Now he is quiet as a mouse

Humpty Dumpty was big and fat
And fell off his walker
They gave him new hips and knees
But he will always be a squawker

Little Jack Horner sat in his corner
Eating his curds and whey
Little Bo Peep has lost her sheep
Now she has nothing to say

Twinkle Twinkle little star
I used to wonder where you are
Roses are red and violets still blue
All my childhood rhymes have come true

Un Poeme Pour Murielle

Murielle *ma belle*
Tu es mon coeur
    Tu es mon fleur
        Ma Murielle

Murielle mon amour
    Je suis tres heureux
        Je t'aime beaucoup
            Ma Murielle

Murielle mon cher
    Ce sont les mots que je veux te dire
        Tu es mon ame
            Ma Murielle

Murielle tu fais briller mes yeux
    Je veux entre dans la vie avec toi
        Tu es l' parfum de Dieu
            Ma Murielle

Murielle tu fais voler mon esprit
    C'est ce que je veux dire
        Ce que je veux tu saches
            Je t'adore ma Murielle

Whatever

Once I was beautiful
But I didn't know it
I thought something was the matter with me
Because people would look at me
As if I had a penis on my face
What a Dickhead
Whatever
Or maybe
A vagina instead of a mouth
What a cunt
Whatever

They are just body parts
We told ourselves
Appendages
And We are our pronouns
They are just extensions or entrances
Into Us or We
Or He or She
Into and out of our real self
We can be happier without them
We tell us selves
Whatever

It doesn't matter anymore
Now We can be one and the same
Different or not
Or both or the other
Or neither or neuter
It's a good thing we are not confused anymore
Because we are free
to truly be fluid like water
And/or maybe who we really are, or not
Whatever

Visions and Dreams

Of Island sands in waters glistening
Waves dancing in rhythms like sambas
Turquoise blue and green, shimmering
 incandescent, an aquamarine scene

Visions and dreams of golden domes and shining spires,
Lustrous villas in which to live
Inspired by mountains, rising like cathedrals
from the tranquil sea

Visions and dreams of Bougainvillea and lime green margaritas
Sun filled clouds in sparkling light suspended in azure space
A soft tropical breeze caresses your face
as the sailboats float by at a leisurely pace

Visions and dreams, realized in the beauty of our embrace

Ode to Wild Wolf

In the forest in the dark
Roams a beast with a pounding heart
In the wild deep in the wood
Is it malevolent or misunderstood

Right or wrong is a human sense
So we look for reasons
The wolf is instinctive
Natural like the seasons

And through dreams from the lair
The scent travels through the air
With raging feelings pent
Roams the wild wolf

Gift of Life

In the twilight of the evening
through the black and dark of night
Comes a glimmer then a sparkle
Came the dawn of new morning light

The sun is rising the darkness fading
Birds are flying and singing bright
Angels are landing bringing greetings
Everything will be all right

What a present what a blessing
To greet each new day and the gift of life
Giving thanks for each new morning
Throughout the day and every night

Forever Grateful

Forever grateful am I
for the many gifts I have been given
For all the songs I have played
and for the poems I have written

Forever blessed am I
to look up at the sky
to feel the ground beneath my feet
to see the Love in your eye

How wondrous it is
to feel the Sun on my face
To watch the clouds fly by
to see the stars in the dark of space

Forever thankful am I
to my Mother and my Father
It could have been a lot easier
but could have been a lot harder

How fortunate am I
to meditate on my breath
To enjoy this day of Life
and delay my date with Death

How happy am I
to enjoy my given time
To reflect on the Divine
and share these words of rhyme

Jewels of Life

Flowing moments of closeness kindness
touching holding wearing
on my neck arms and fingers
Priceless jewels strung together on the
line of time
like a necklace of my mind

Precious instances
Of smiling laughter in colors
Like rubies emeralds pearls and aquamarines
Shaped like raindrops wrapped around your wrist
Like a bracelet of the heart

Glistening golden is the early morning light
The sun reflecting the turning autumnal leaves
Love beams like diamonds from your eyes
Enveloping like a ring of the soul
The jewels of life

Until

I have been to Monaco and Acapulco
     Amalfi and Capri too
But I have never been anywhere
     Until I just met you

I have journeyed to Paris, Milan,
     Tuscany Rome and Corfu
Seen the David the Mona Lisa
     Musee Picasso and Dali too
But I have never seen anything
     Until I just saw you

I have climbed mountain tops
     And hills of morning dew
And I have swum the Atlantic, the Pacific
     And the Mediterranean too
But I have never swum anywhere
     Until I swam to you

I have lived in forests and deserts
     On seaside cliffs so blue
In cities countries and jungles
     So many places I have been it's true
But I have never been anywhere
     Until I have been with you

I could be anywhere at any time or any place
Just so I could be close enough
To gaze upon your face
I would be under the darkest cloud
Or under sunny skies
Just to be close enough
To look into your eyes

Ode to Fortune

Fortune has again called upon me
Life has thrown me another curveball
And I am leaving my comfortable country home
My forest dwelling, my mountain lodge my nature retreat
 sprinkled with farms hills fields and streams

I am emerging from my chrysalis like a winged dragon
 flying into the distance of an unknown dream

Goodbye to country fairs and fall harvest festivals
Bake sales, fresh apple pies and cinnamon laced hot cider
Brilliant fall foliage and crisp evenings
 by the warmth of a crackling fire

Farewell to Spring buds and the yellow blooms of daffodil and forsythia
Adieu to fresh snowfall in a winter wonderland blessed by scarlet
cardinals
Adios to Christmas displays of jolly snowmen with gifts in sleighs
 and Sayonara to long hot sweaty summer days

Yes. I am moving on for a new life on the great ship of destiny
And set sail into the forever sunset on the ocean of eternity
to greet each new sunrise and grow in the glow of the eternal sun
I will soar in the breeze of tropical winds and listen to the siren song
 of the waves lulling me to sleep

Forever young beautiful and carefree
To live Life with my golden queen in splendor and harmony
Together and forever in Love as one
And reincarnate as Apollo, god of the sun

Ode to a Wanderer

Have you seen him
He was just here and now he's gone
He comes and goes with the breeze
the free wind is his song

We all know him as a wanderer
but all who wander are not lost
To those few who embrace life to its fullness
regardless of the cost

He is a traveler through time and space and
known by many in many a different place

He could be the silver surfer riding through the stars
or a holy saint nailed to a cross

He could be the Buddha sitting on the street
but you may not recognize him should you meet

You may notice him by the shine in his eyes or the look of his face
He may be very near or some far off place
He may seem familiar as if you had known him before
or maybe he is a being from the future or from the days of yore

He might be blessed but you may see him as cursed
You may think of him as the best or possibly the worst
He might be fondly remembered or soon and quickly forgotten
you may think of him as loving and sweet or bitter and rotten

He is known to many by many different names
but his true nature is always the same

He is known as the wanderer
But all who wander are not lost
You may have met him
if your stars have crossed

Ode to Beauty

Throughout time many have searched
For beauty and the mythical Fountain of Youth
More fortunate are those who seek their source
and drink from the Fountain of Truth
Some may search for beauty in a bottle
Believing they can perpetuate their looks forever
While those who know that the truth within
is the source of the most precious treasure
Beauty surely has its moment in the sun
But even the most fragrantly scented flower
Withers and wilts, as the brilliance of the day
slowly fades, and the setting sun loses its power
Beauty is not to be found at the elusive fountain of youth
But revealed to those who tread the path in search of their inner truth
True beauty is ethereal, eternal and can never grow faint or fade
A *thing of beauty is a joy forever* it is heavenly and divinely made

Note: A *thing of beauty is a joy forever* is from the John Keats poem,
"Endymion"

About the Author

Samuel Gluck was born August 18, 1947, to an eastern European immigrant family and raised in The Bronx and Yonkers, New York. He attended the University of Bridgeport and graduated with a bachelor of arts degree in history in 1970.

Sam had a 45-year career in financial services. He was an adjunct professor at Pace University in New York, where he taught yoga and meditation for 45 years. He also taught classes, courses, and workshops throughout the New York area.

His first poem, included herein, is *Island Lady*, which he wrote in 1970 and which was published in 1994 in "A Far Off Place" by the National Library of Poetry. Since then, his poems have been published in various anthologies. His first collection, "Muse," was released earlier in 2025.

Sam's inspiration and muse is nature, which is his home, love, which has been his blessing, and God, the source of his being.

Visit samuelgluckpoet.com for more.

About Orenaug Mountain Publishing (OMP)

It is the vision of Orenaug Mountain Publishing (www.orenaugmountainpublishing.com) to be a beacon for poetic expression and to create a platform for poets to share their work with the world.

We seek to champion the art of poetry of writers around the world by publishing high-quality work that challenges, inspires, and connects readers to the human experience.

We do this through several themed anthology projects a year and via the online Orenaug Mountain Poetry Journal at www.orenaugmountainpoetry.net.

Visit our website to learn more about what we do, and to find out how to take part in our anthologies or our poetry journal.

www.ingramcontent.com/pod-product-compliance
Lightning Source LLC
Chambersburg PA
CBHW080520090426
42734CB00015B/3120